Englisch: sehr gut

junior

3. Klasse

Birgit Kölmel

Mit Download für phase-6 *junior*

In Zusammenarbeit
mit Langenscheidt

mentor
Eine Klasse besser.

Die Autorin:
Birgit Kölmel ist als Grund- und Hauptschullehrerin in Baden-Württemberg sowie als Autorin verschiedener Lernhilfen tätig.

Projektbetreuung: Alexandra Bauer für bookwise medienproduktion GmbH, München
Redaktion: Doris Nathrath, München
Layout: Regina Rechter, München
Umschlaggestaltung: Design im Kontor – Iris Steiner, München
Illustrationen: Ute Ohlms, Braunschweig

Umwelthinweis: Gedruckt auf chlorfrei gebleichtem Papier.

Satz: Daniel Förster, Belgern

Printed in Germany
ISBN 978-3-580-65223-4

10010

Inhalt

Hallo liebe Schülerin, hallo lieber Schüler,

wir beide werden dich gemeinsam durch dieses Buch begleiten.

Suri ist ein Erdmännchen und kommt aus Afrika.

Wir sind schon lange die besten Freunde und haben bereits zahlreiche aufregende Abenteuer miteinander erlebt.

Gemeinsam mit uns kannst du in diesem Buch alles lernen, was für Englisch in der 3. Klasse wichtig ist. Damit dir das auch richtig Spaß macht, haben wir uns viele Rätsel und jede Menge abwechslungsreiche Übungen ausgedacht.

Außerdem findest du in diesem Buch drei Tests. Hier kannst du selbst herausfinden, was du schon gelernt hast und wo du nochmals üben solltest.

Für jede Testaufgabe gibt es eine bestimmte Anzahl an Punkten. Löse die Aufgaben, ohne im Buch nachzuschauen, und sieh erst danach in die Lösungen.

Dann kannst du die erreichten Punkte in deinen Test eintragen – oder du bittest einen Erwachsenen, deine Aufgaben nachzuprüfen und dir die entsprechenden Punkte zu geben. In der Testauswertung auf Seite 87 erfährst du dann, wie gut du den Test geschafft hast.

Viel Erfolg und Spaß beim Üben wünschen dir

Jule und Suri

Englisch ist eine wichtige Sprache, die von vielen Menschen auf der ganzen Welt gesprochen wird. In diesem Buch lernst du unter anderem, wie man sich auf Englisch begrüßt, wie man bis zwanzig zählt und wie die Wochentage heißen.

Bei den Übungen findest du folgende Zeichen, die dir zeigen, was zu tun ist:

 Kreise ein!

 Verbinde!

 Fülle aus! / Schreibe auf!

 Male! / Male an!

 Sprich auf Englisch!

1 HELLO!

Hello!
Hey!
My name is …
I'm from Germany.
I'm from Africa.

Spain
France
Great Britain
Germany
Italy

Exercise 1

Hello!
My name is Jule.
I'm from Germany.

Hallo! Ich heiße Jule.
Ich komme aus
Deutschland.

Hey!
My name is Suri.
I'm from Africa.

Hallo! Ich heiße Suri.
Ich komme aus Afrika.

Exercise 2

My name is …

My name is …

- ❏ My name is Jule.
- ❏ My name is Suri.
- ❏ My name is Anna.

- ❏ My name is Tom.
- ❏ My name is Jule.
- ❏ My name is Suri.

I'm from …

I'm from …

- ❏ I'm from Africa.
- ❏ I'm from Germany.

- ❏ I'm from Germany.
- ❏ I'm from Africa.

Exercise 3

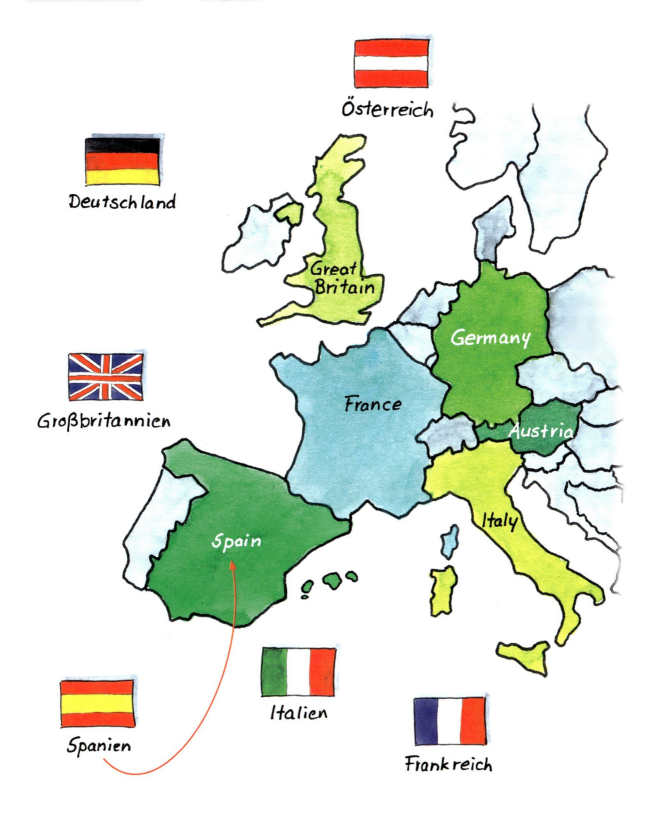

Exercise 4

Und nun bist du dran: Zeichne dein Gesicht in einen Bilderrahmen.
In den anderen Bilderrahmen kannst du deine beste Freundin oder
deinen besten Freund malen.

Talk to your partner. (Sprich mit deinem Partner.)

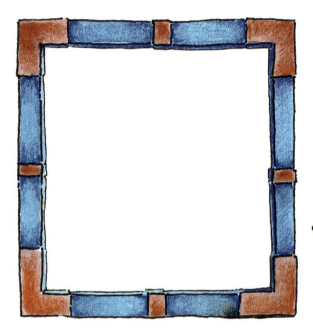

Hello!
My ... is ... .
I'm from ... .

Hey!
My ... is ... .
I'm from ... .

2 FAMILY

mother   sister   this is my …
father   brother   his name is …
grandmother   grandfather   her name is …

Exercise 1

brother

grandfather

mother

grandmother

father

sister

11

Exercise 2

- ❏ brother
- ❏ father
- ❏ grandfather

- ❏ sister
- ❏ mother
- ❏ grandmother

- ❏ mother
- ❏ sister
- ❏ grandmother

- ❏ father
- ❏ brother
- ❏ grandfather

Exercise 3

father

This is my _____ .

His name is Peter.

mother

This is my _____ .

Her name is Anne.

brother

And this is my _____ .

His name is Kevin.

Exercise 4

My family

mother

father

brother

sister

grandfather

grandmother

3 AT HOME

Where is the ...?

house	bath
window	bed
living room	table
bedroom	chair
bathroom	lamp
kitchen	sofa

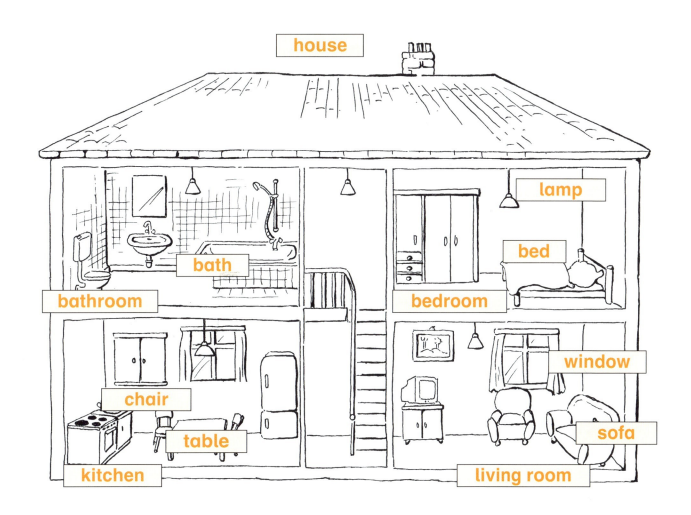

Exercise 1

Look at page 15. Fill in the words.
(Schaue auf Seite 15. Trage die Wörter ein.)

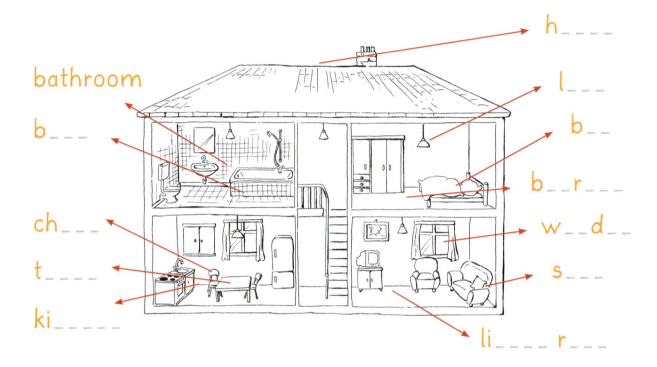

bathroom

b _ _ _

ch _ _ _ _

t _ _ _ _

ki _ _ _ _ _

h _ _ _ _ _

l _ _ _

b _ _

b _ _ r _ _ _

w _ _ d _ _

s _ _ _

li _ _ _ _ r _ _

Exercise 2

Colour in the house on page 15. (Male das Haus auf Seite 15 an.)

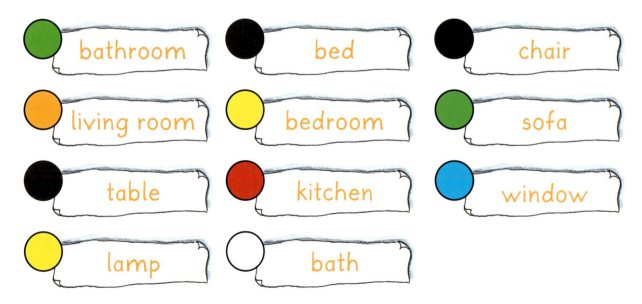

bathroom

bed

chair

living room

bedroom

sofa

table

kitchen

window

lamp

bath

Exercise 3

Where is Max?
(Wo ist Max?)

- ❏ Max is in the kitchen.
- ❏ Max is in the bathroom.
- ❏ Max is in the bedroom.

Where is father?

- ❏ Father is in the living room.
- ❏ Father is in the bathroom.
- ❏ Father is in the kitchen.

Where is mother?

- ❏ Mother is in the living room.
- ❏ Mother is in the bathroom.
- ❏ Mother is in the bedroom.

4 AT SCHOOL

I've got…

pencil	book
school bag	ruler
pencil case	rubber
pen	glue

Exercise 1

pencil case

rubber

pen

ruler

book

school bag

pencil

glue

Exercise 2

pencil
pencil case
rubber
ruler

pen
pencil case
book
glue

Exercise 3

Talk to your partner.

Legt zuerst alle abgebildeten
Gegenstände bereit. Dann übernimmt
einer die Rolle von Jule und bittet
auf Englisch um einen Gegenstand.
Ein anderer spielt Suri und reicht das
Gewünschte. Sprecht dabei laut und
tauscht die Rollen.

Exercise 4

Exercise 5

I've got…

❑ …a rubber.
❑ …a book.
❑ …a school bag.

I've got…

❑ …a ruler.
❑ …a pencil.
❑ …a pencil case.

I've got…

❑ …a glue.
❑ …a pen.
❑ …a school bag.

Stand up, please.
Sit down, please.
Open your book, please.
Close your book, please.

Clean the board, please.
Be quiet, please.
door
board

Exercise 6

Close your _____, please.

Open the _____, please.

Stand _____, please.

Be _____, please.

23

Exercise 7

Stand up, please.

Sit down, please.

Open your book, please.

Close your book, please.

Be quiet, please.

Open the window, please.

Close the door, please.

Clean the board, please.

Exercise 8

Open the window, please.

Close the door, please.

Clean the board, please.

Be quiet, please.

Am besten machst du erst die Kärtchen bei phase-6 junior!

TEST

Meine Punkte in diesem Test: ☐

Do you remember? (Erinnerst du dich?)

Lösung: Seite 72

Exercise 1

Bei **Exercise 1** habe ich ☐ von 2 Punkten.

Hello!

My name is _____ .

I'm from _____ .

Exercise 2

Bei **Exercise 2** habe ich ☐ von 4 Punkten.

❑ bathroom
❑ living room

❑ bedroom
❑ kitchen

❑ bedroom
❑ kitchen

❑ bathroom
❑ living room

Exercise 3

Bei **Exercise 3** habe ich ☐ von 2 Punkten.

❑ mother
❑ grandmother

❑ sister
❑ grandfather

Exercise 4

Bei **Exercise 4** habe ich ☐ von 2 Punkten.

chair

bed

Exercise 5

Bei **Exercise 5** habe ich ☐ von 5 Punkten.

window

rubber

book

ruler

house

pencil case

pencil

~~kitchen~~

pen

5 NUMBERS

1	2	3	4	5	6	7	8	9	10
one	two	three	four	five	six	seven	eight	nine	ten

Exercise 1

Exercise 2

📞 one-three-eight-two-one

1 - 3 _____

📞 five-four-nine-seven-six

_____

Exercise 3

 two _____

_____

_____

> Hmmmm!
> I like eggs.

_____

Exercise 4

I've got eight balls.

I've got three bananas.

I've got seven books.

I've got one brother.

Exercise 5

three + one   =   *four*

nine − six   =   _____

ten   − three =   _____

four + six   =   _____

eight − seven =   _____

four + four =   _____

nine − four =   _____

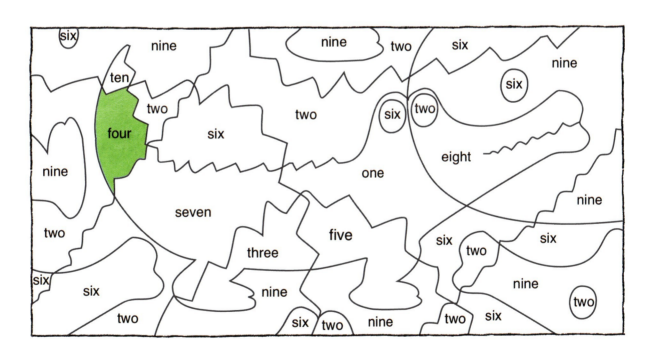

Numbers

11	12	13	14	15
eleven	twelve	thirteen	fourteen	fifteen

16	17	18	19	20
sixteen	seventeen	eighteen	nineteen	twenty

Exercise 6

   t _ _ l _ e   t h _ _ t _ _ n

   f _ _ _ _ _ n   

   e i _ _ t _ _ _   n _ _ _ _ e _ _

Exercise 7

A	E	L	E	V	E	N	N
S	A	C	V	R	L	W	X
F	O	U	R	T	E	E	N
N	I	N	E	T	E	E	N
K	K	I	I	V	O	U	R
F	I	F	T	E	E	N	Y
O	J	T	W	E	N	T	Y

eleven   11

four   4

nineteen   19

fifteenn   15

twenty   18

Exercise 8

How old are you? Ask your partner. (Wie alt bist du? Frage deinen Partner.)

I'm nine.

I'm two.

I'm _____ .

I'm _____ .

6 COLOURS

white   black ⚫   yellow   red 🔴

green 🟢   blue 🔵   brown 🟤   orange 🟠

Exercise 1

Exercise 2

GREENWHITEYELLOWBROWNREDBLACKBLUEORANGE

green _____

_____

_____

_____

_____

_____

_____

_____

Exercise 3

❑ The book is black.
❑ The book is blue.

❑ The pencil is red.
❑ The pencil is brown.

❑ The pen is green.
❑ The pen is yellow.

❑ The rubber is red and orange.
❑ The rubber is blue and white.

Exercise 4

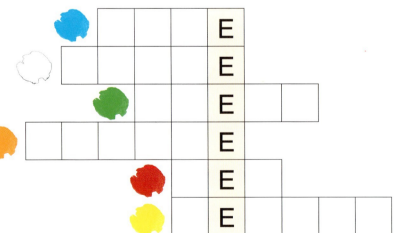

7 FOOD

banana   apple   melon
tomato   orange   potato
egg   chocolate   bread
ice cream

Exercise 1

- ☒ yellow
- ☐ blue
- ☒ banana

- ☐ black
- ☐ red
- ☐ tomato

- ☐ green
- ☐ brown
- ☐ bread

- ☐ yellow
- ☐ white
- ☐ egg

- ☐ blue
- ☐ red
- ☐ melon

- ☐ green
- ☐ white
- ☐ apple

Exercise 2

potato

egg

melon

ice cream

chocolate

apple

Exercise 3

D	E	E	J	Y	M	K	E	T
T	N	D	S	W	E	Z	B	R
C	H	O	C	O	L	A	T	E
E	O	R	A	N	G	E	E	N
A	P	P	L	E	V	Q	G	N
P	L	B	R	E	A	D	G	N
J	M	E	L	O	N	C	J	O
C	M	M	P	O	T	A	T	O

chocolate

or

ap

me

br

po

eg

Exercise 4

Talk to your partner.

Spiele Kaufen und Verkaufen auf Englisch. Lege zuerst die abgebildeten Lebensmittel bereit. Dann spielt einer den Verkäufer, ein anderer den Käufer. Weißt du noch, was der Verkäufer jedes Mal sagt, wenn er das Gewünschte reicht?

Can I have the apple, please? Thank you.

Exercise 5

Thank you for …

…the apple.
…the bread.
…the egg.
…the chocolate.

8 DRINKS

a cup of tea

a cup of coffee

a bottle of milk

a bottle of water

a cup of hot chocolate

a bottle of lemonade

a bottle of orange juice

a bottle of apple juice

hot

cold

Exercise 1

a cup of hot chocolate

a bottle of milk

a cup of tea

a bottle of orange juice

a bottle of water

Drinks

Exercise 2

a bottle of

a cup of hot

a bottle of

a bottle of

a bottle of

a cup of

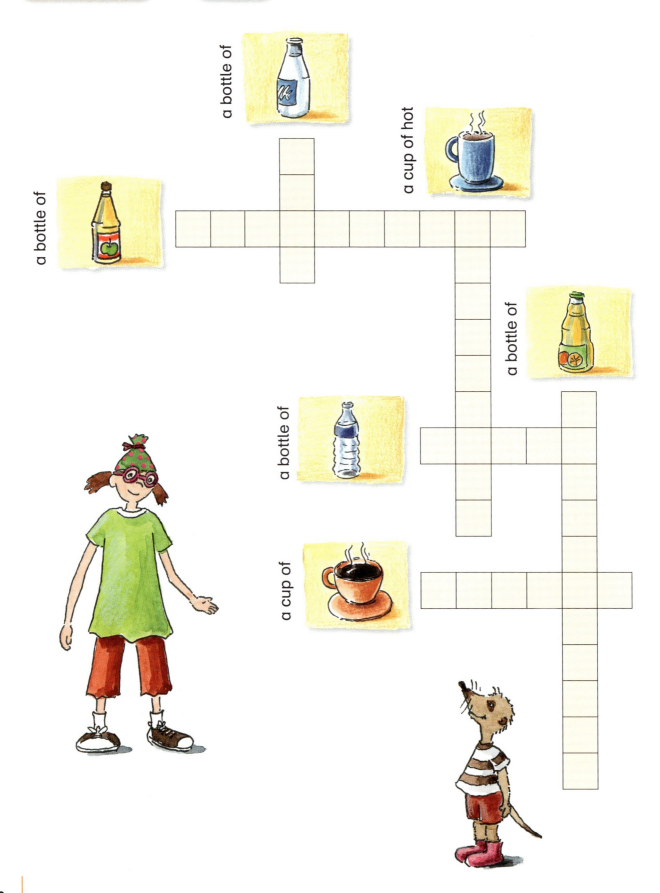

Exercise 3

a) It's white.

- ☒ milk
- ☐ coffee
- ☐ orange juice

b) It's yellow.

- ☐ milk
- ☐ orange juice
- ☐ water

c) It's brown.

- ☐ orange juice
- ☐ coffee
- ☐ hot chocolate

d) It's cold.

- ☐ coffee
- ☐ lemonade
- ☐ hot chocolate

Exercise 4

I like …
And what about you?

 I like milk.

 I like

 I like

 I like

Exercise 5

hot drinks	cold drinks
a cup of coffee	a bottle of milk
a bottle of lemonade	a cup of hot chocolate
a bottle of orange juice	a bottle of apple juice
a cup of tea	a bottle of water

Exercise 6

a cup of eta

a bottle of nadelemo

a bottle of klmi

a cup of hot latechoco

a bottle of orange cejui

a cup of coeeff

Am besten machst du erst die Kärtchen bei phase-6 junior!

TEST

Meine Punkte in diesem Test: ☐

Do you remember? (Erinnerst du dich?)　　　　Lösung: Seite 79

Exercise 1

Bei **Exercise 1** habe ich ☐ von 5 Punkten.

 one _____　 _____

 _____　 _____　 _____

Exercise 2

Bei **Exercise 2** habe ich ☐ von 3 Punkten.

erd　red _____

lbue _____

lback _____

rgeen _____

Exercise 3

Bei **Exercise 3** habe ich ☐ von 4 Punkten.

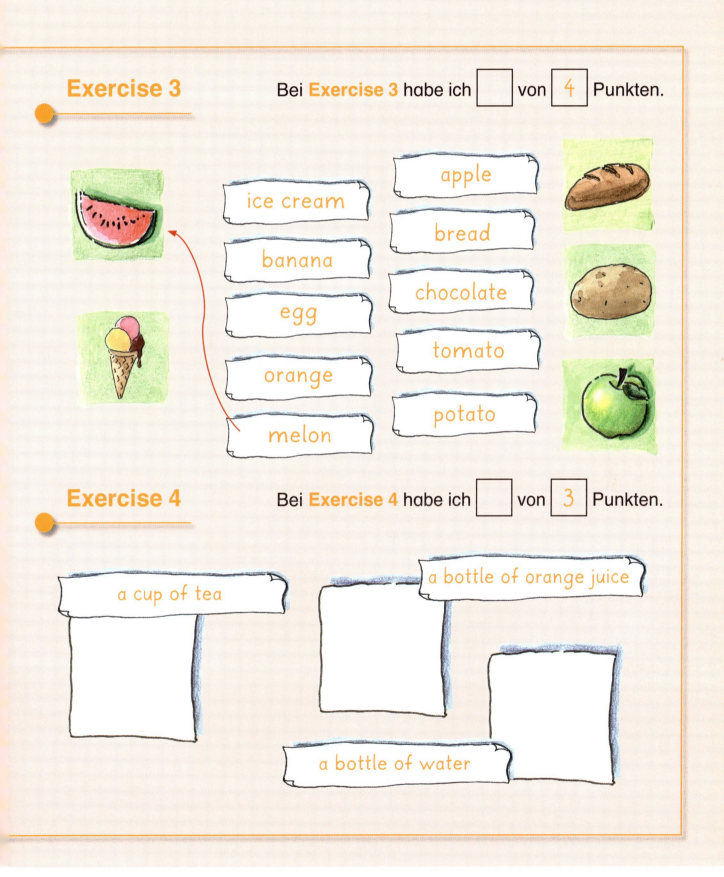

ice cream

banana

egg

orange

melon

apple

bread

chocolate

tomato

potato

Exercise 4

Bei **Exercise 4** habe ich ☐ von 3 Punkten.

a cup of tea

a bottle of orange juice

a bottle of water

9 ANIMALS

pig	dog	cat
chicken	sheep	bird
cow	horse	goose

Exercise 1

pig

sheep

chicken

cow

horse

cat

dog

goose

bird

Exercise 2

❑ sheep   ❑ bird   ❑ cat   ❑ dog   ❑ goose   ❑ bird

❑ horse   ❑ pig   ❑ sheep   ❑ horse   ❑ pig   ❑ cow

Exercise 3

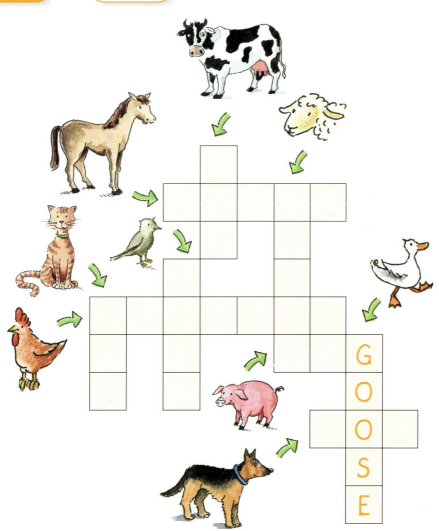

Exercise 4

The horse is _brown_____.

The goose is _____.

The _____.

The _____

is _____

and _____.

The _____.

The _____

is _____

and _____.

Exercise 5

Look at page 48. Can you find the four missing animals?

(Schau auf Seite 48. Kannst du die vier fehlenden Tiere finden?)

Exercise 6

Exercise 7

sheep

sheep

pig

dog

bird

cat

chicken

10 DAYS OF THE WEEK

Monday
Tuesday
Wednesday
Thursday
Friday
Saturday
Sunday

every
I'm together with …
I watch TV
I play
we go shopping

Exercise 1

Mon	Monday	Monday
Tue	Tuesday	
Wed	Wednesday	
Thurs	Thursday	
Fri	Friday	
Sat	Saturday	
Sun	Sunday	

Exercise 2

1 — Mon d a y

2 — Tues _____

3 — Wednes _____

4 — Th _____ day

5 — _____ day

6 — _____ day

7 — _____

Wochentage werden groß-geschrieben!

Exercise 3

What do you do on Monday?

Every Monday I play football.

Every **Monday** I play football.

Every **T** I'm together with my grandmother.

Every _____ I watch TV.

Every _____ I'm together with Jule.

Every _____ I play the piano.

Every _____ we go shopping.

Every _____ I'm together with my family.

Exercise 4

And what about Tom? (Und wie ist es bei Tom?)

Every Monday
I watch TV.

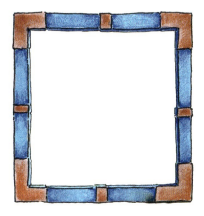

Every Tuesday
I'm together with
my sister.

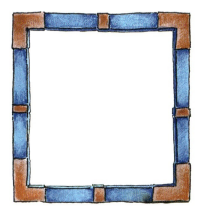

Every Wednesday
I go shopping with
my mother.

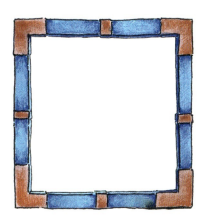

Every Thursday
I play football.

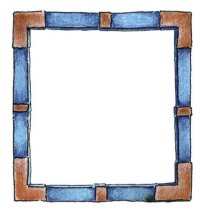

Every Friday
I'm together with
my friend Robin.

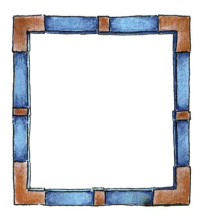

Every Saturday
I play the piano.

Exercise 5

Every | Tuesday | I'm | together | with | my | grandmother.

EveryWednesdayIwatchTVtogetherwithSuri.

EveryMondayIplayfootball.

EverySaturdaywegoshopping.

Exercise 6

| Sonntag | | | | D | |

| Donnerstag | | | | | D | |

| Freitag | | | | D | |

| Dienstag | | | | D | |

| Mittwoch | | D | | | | | |

| Montag | | | | D | |

| Samstag | | | | D | |

11 TIME

What time is it?
What's the time?
It's three o'clock.

Exercise 1

a) It's eight o'clock.

b) It's _____ o'clock.

c) It's _____ o'clock.

d) It's _____ o'clock.

 **Exercise 2**

It's six o'clock.

It's one o'clock.

It's ten o'clock.

It's four o'clock.

 Exercise 3

Talk to your partner.

Spiele die Situation mit deinem Partner. Einer fragt nach der Uhrzeit. Der andere antwortet mit einer Zeit, die hier abgebildet ist. Dann tauscht ihr die Rollen.

What time is it?

It's five o'clock.

Exercise 4

It's two o'clock.

It's five o'clock.

It's seven o'clock.

It's nine o'clock.

It's eleven o'clock.

It's twelve o'clock.

It's _three o'_ _____.

It's _____.

Exercise 5

Exercise 6

What time is it?

- ❏ It's eleven o'clock.
- ❏ It's one o'clock.
- ❏ It's twelve o'clock.

- ❏ It's two o'clock.
- ❏ It's three o'clock.
- ❏ It's four o'clock.

- ❏ It's ten o'clock.
- ❏ It's nine o'clock.
- ❏ It's eleven o'clock.

Am besten machst du erst die Kärtchen bei phase-6 junior!

TEST

Meine Punkte in diesem Test: [ ]

Do you remember? (Erinnerst du dich?)   Lösung: Seite 85

Exercise 1

Bei **Exercise 1** habe ich [ ] von [4] Punkten.

☐ pig
☐ bird

☐ goose
☐ sheep

☐ dog
☐ horse

☐ cat
☐ cow

Exercise 2

Bei **Exercise 2** habe ich [ ] von [3] Punkten.

a brown h___rse

a red b____rd

a yellow ch___cken

TEST

Exercise 3

Bei **Exercise 3** habe ich ☐ von 6 Punkten.

Mon ➜ Monday

Tue ➜ _____

Wed ➜ _____

Thurs ➜ _____

Fri ➜ _____

Sat ➜ _____

Sun ➜ _____

Exercise 4

Bei **Exercise 4** habe ich ☐ von 3 Punkten.

It's seven o'clock.

It's ten o'clock.

It's one o'clock.

It's five o'clock.

LÖSUNGEN

1 HELLO!

Exercise 1 Seite 7

Sprich die Sätze mehrmals laut, am besten mit deinen Eltern oder Freunden.

Exercise 2 Seite 8

My name is Jule.

My name is Suri.

I'm from Germany.

I'm from Africa.

Exercise 3 Seite 9

Exercise 4 Seite 10

Spiele das Vorstellen auf Englisch in deiner Familie oder mit deinen Freunden. Wenn es dir schwerfällt, dann übe so lange, bis es einfacher wird.

2 FAMILY

Exercise 1 — Seite 11

father

brother

mother

grandmother

sister

grandfather

Exercise 2 — Seite 12

grandfather

sister

mother

brother

Exercise 3 — Seite 13

This is my father.
His name is Peter.

This is my mother.
Her name is Anne.

And this is my brother.
His name is Kevin.

Exercise 4 — Seite 14

Sind dir die Bilder gut gelungen?
Wenn du möchtest, kannst du sie deiner Familie zeigen.

3 AT HOME

Exercise 1 Seite 16

(links)	(rechts)
bathroom	house
bath	lamp
chair	bed
table	bedroom
kitchen	window
	sofa
	living room

Exercise 2 Seite 16

Sieh nochmals nach, ob du das Haus in den richtigen Farben angemalt hast:

Wohnzimmer – orange
Schlafzimmer – gelb
Küche – rot
Badezimmer – grün
Badewanne – weiß
Lampe – gelb
Bett – schwarz
Tisch – schwarz
Stuhl – schwarz
Fenster – blau
Sofa – grün

Exercise 3 Seite 17

Max is in the bathroom.

Father is in the kitchen.

Mother is in the living room.

4 AT SCHOOL

Exercise 1   Seite 18

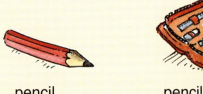

pencil   pencil case

book   ruler   glue

rubber   school bag

Exercise 2   Seite 19
Diese Schulsachen solltest du in Suris
Ranzen eingeordnet haben: Füller,
Mäppchen, Buch, Kleber.
Diese Schulsachen solltest du in Jules
Mäppchen eingeordnet haben: Bleistift,
Mäppchen, Radiergummi, Lineal.

Exercise 3   Seite 20
Folgende Gegenstände solltest du
erwähnt haben: pencil case, book, rubber,
glue, school bag, pencil, ruler, pen.

Exercise 4   Seite 21

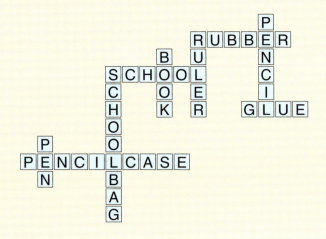

Exercise 5   Seite 22

I've got a book.

I've got a pencil case.

I've got a glue.

Exercise 6   Seite 23

Close your book, please.

Open the window, please.

Stand up, please.

Be quiet, please.

Exercise 7   Seite 24

Stand up, please.

Open your book, please.

Be quiet, please.

Close the door, please.

Sit down, please.

Close your book, please.

Open the window, please.

Clean the board, please.

Exercise 8   Seite 25

Close the door, please.

Clean the board, please.

Be quiet, please.

TEST

Höchstpunktzahl: **15 Punkte**

Exercise 1   Seite 26
Zähle für jedes richtige Wort **1 Punkt**.
My name is Jule. I'm from Germany.

Exercise 2   Seite 26
Zähle für jedes richtig angekreuzte
Wort **1 Punkt**.
Oben links – bathroom, oben rechts –
bedroom, unten links – kitchen, unten
rechts – living room

Exercise 3   Seite 27
Zähle für jedes richtig angekreuzte
Wort **1 Punkt**.
mother (links)   grandfather (rechts)

Exercise 4   Seite 27
Zähle für jedes richtig gemalte Bild
1 Punkt.
Links: In diesen Rahmen solltest du
einen Stuhl gezeichnet haben.
Rechts: In diesen Rahmen solltest du
ein Bett gezeichnet haben.

Exercise 5   Seite 27
Zähle für jedes richtig eingeordnete
Wort **1 Punkt**.
Diese Wörter solltest du in den
Schulranzen packen: pen, pencil
case, book, ruler, rubber.

5 NUMBERS

Exercise 1   Seite 28
Diese Paare solltest du mit der gleichen
Farbe angemalt haben:
one – 1, two – 2, three – 3, four – 4,
five – 5, six – 6, seven – 7, eight – 8,
nine – 9, ten – 10

Exercise 2   Seite 29
Suri: 1 – 3 – 8 – 2 – 1
Jule: 5 – 4 – 9 – 7 – 6

Exercise 3   Seite 29
2 Eier – two eggs, 9 Eier – nine eggs,
7 Eier – seven eggs, 5 Eier – five eggs

Exercise 4   Seite 30

I've got three bananas.

I've got seven books.

I've got one brother.

Exercise 5 Seite 31

three + one = four
nine – six = three
ten – three = seven
four + six = ten
eight – seven = one
four + four = eight
nine – four = five

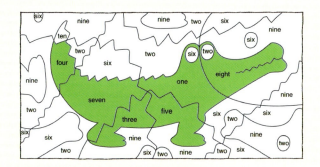

Exercise 6 Seite 32

eleven – twelve – thirteen
fourteen – fifteen – sixteen
seventeen – eighteen – nineteen
twenty

Exercise 7 Seite 33

eleven	11
fourteen	14
fifteen	15
nineteen	19
twenty	20

A	E	L	E	V	E	N	N
S	A	C	V	R	L	W	X
F	O	U	R	T	E	E	N
N	I	N	E	T	E	E	N
K	K	I	I	V	O	U	R
F	I	F	T	E	E	N	Y
O	J	T	W	E	N	T	Y

Exercise 8 Seite 33

I'm nine.

I'm two.

I'm eleven.

I'm ten.

Vielleicht sind deine Freunde in einem anderen Alter? Schaue am besten im Buch nach, ob du die Zahlwörter richtig geschrieben hast.

6 COLOURS

Exercise 1   Seite 34

Sicher hast du die Ballons richtig
angemalt.

Exercise 2   Seite 35

grüner Klecks – green
weißer Klecks – white
gelber Klecks – yellow
brauner Klecks – brown
roter Klecks – red
schwarzer Klecks – black
blauer Klecks – blue
orangefarbener Klecks – orange

Exercise 3   Seite 36

The book is blue.

The pencil is red.

The pen is green.

The rubber is blue
and white.

Exercise 4   Seite 36

		B	L	U	E		
	W	H	I	T	E		
			G	R	E	E	N
O	R	A	N	G	E		
				R	E	D	
			Y	E	L	L	O	W

7 FOOD

Exercise 1 Seite 37

a) yellow, banana
b) red, tomato
c) brown, bread
d) white, egg
e) red, melon
f) green, apple

Exercise 2 Seite 38

Exercise 3 Seite 39

chocolate, orange, apple, melon, bread, potato, egg

D	E	E	J	Y	M	K	E	T
T	N	D	S	W	E	Z	B	R
C	H	O	C	O	L	A	T	E
E	O	R	A	N	G	E	E	N
A	P	P	L	E	V	Q	G	N
P	L	B	R	E	A	D	G	N
J	M	E	L	O	N	C	J	O
C	M	M	P	O	T	A	T	O

Exercise 4 Seite 39

Nach folgenden Lebensmitteln solltest du als Käufer gefragt haben: egg, bread, melon, banana, tomato, potato.
Der Verkäufer sagt dann immer: Here you are. Das kennst du schon aus Kapitel 4, Exercise 3.

Exercise 5

Seite 40

8 DRINKS

Exercise 1 Seite 41

a bottle of orange juice

a cup of tea

a bottle of milk

a bottle of water

a cup of hot chocolate

Exercise 2 Seite 42

Exercise 3 Seite 43

a) It's white: milk.

b) It's yellow: orange juice.

c) It's brown: coffee, hot chocolate.

d) It's cold: lemonade.

Exercise 4 Seite 43

I like hot chocolate.

I like orange juice.

I like water.

Exercise 5   Seite 44

a cup of coffee
a bottle of lemonade
a bottle of orange juice
a cup of tea

a bottle of milk
a cup of hot chocolate
a bottle of apple juice
a bottle of water

Exercise 6   Seite 45

a cup of tea
(eine Tasse Tee)
a bottle of lemonade
(eine Flasche Limonade)
a bottle of milk
(eine Flasche Milch)
a cup of hot chocolate
(eine Tasse heiße Schokolade)
a bottle of orange juice
(eine Flasche Orangensaft)
a cup of coffee
(eine Tasse Kaffee)

TEST

Höchstpunktzahl: **15 Punkte**

Exercise 1 Seite 46
Zähle für jede richtige Zahl **1 Punkt**.

one	three	ten
two	six	four

Exercise 2 Seite 46
Zähle für jede richtige Farbe +
englisches Wort **1 Punkt**.
b) blue – blau
c) black – schwarz
d) green – grün

Exercise 3 Seite 47
Zähle für jede richtige Zuordnung
1 Punkt.

melon

ice cream

bread

potato

apple

Exercise 4 Seite 47
Zähle für jedes richtig gemalte Bild
1 Punkt.
Dies solltest du jeweils in die Rahmen
gezeichnet haben:
a) eine Tasse Tee
b) eine Flasche Orangensaft
c) eine Flasche Wasser

9 ANIMALS

Exercise 1   Seite 48

Exercise 2   Seite 49

sheep, pig, cat, horse, goose, bird

The horse is brown.

The goose is white.

The chicken is brown (and red).

Exercise 3   Seite 49

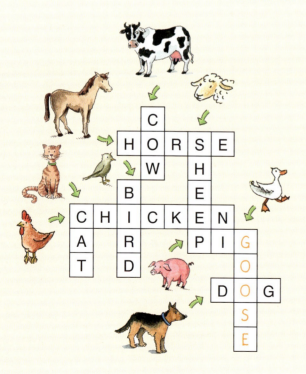

The cow is black and white.

The sheep is white.

The dog is brown and black.

Exercise 5   Seite 51

pig – goose – cat – chicken

Exercise 6   Seite 52

woof-woof

peep-peep

oink-oink

moo-moo

Exercise 7   Seite 53

sheep   pig

dog   bird

cat   chicken

81

10 DAYS OF THE WEEK

Exercise 1 Seite 54

Mon – Monday
Tue – Tuesday
Wed – Wednesday
Thurs – Thursday
Fri – Friday
Sat – Saturday
Sun – Sunday

Every Thursday I'm together with Jule.

Exercise 2 Seite 55

Monday, Tuesday, Wednesday,
Thursday, Friday, Saturday, Sunday

Every Friday I play the piano.

Exercise 3 Seite 56

Every Tuesday I'm together with my grandmother.

Every Saturday we go shopping.

Every Wednesday I watch TV.

Every Sunday I'm together with my family.

Exercise 4   Seite 57

Hier die Übersetzung auf Deutsch.
Sieh noch mal nach, ob du alles richtig
verstanden und gezeichnet hast.

- Every Monday I watch TV. – Jeden
  Montag sehe ich fern.
- Every Tuesday I'm together with my
  sister. – Jeden Dienstag bin ich mit
  meiner Schwester zusammen.
- Every Wednesday I go shopping with
  my mother. – Jeden Mittwoch gehe ich
  mit meiner Mutter einkaufen.
- Every Thursday I play football. – Jeden
  Donnerstag spiele ich Fußball.
- Every Friday I'm together with my
  friend Robin. – Jeden Freitag bin ich
  mit meinem Freund Robin zusammen.
- Every Saturday I play the piano. –
  Jeden Samstag spiele ich Klavier.

Every / Monday / I / play / football.

Every / Saturday / we / go / shopping.

Exercise 5   Seite 58

Every / Wednesday / I / watch / TV /
together / with / Suri.

Exercise 6   Seite 59

Sonntag → S U N D A Y
Donnerstag → T H U R S D A Y
Freitag → F R I D A Y
Dienstag → T U E S D A Y
Mittwoch → W E D N E S D A Y
Montag → M O N D A Y
Samstag → S A T U R D A Y

11 TIME

Exercise 1 — Seite 60

a) It's eight o'clock.
b) It's one o'clock.
c) It's ten o'clock.
d) It's seven o'clock.

Exercise 2 — Seite 61

 It's six o'clock.

 It's one o'clock.

 It's ten o'clock.

 It's four o'clock.

Exercise 3 — Seite 61

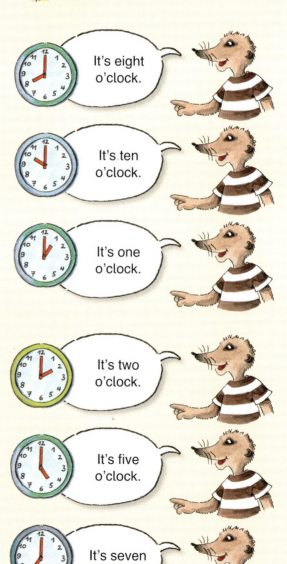

Exercise 4 Seite 62

It's two o'clock.
It's five o'clock.
It's seven o'clock.
It's nine o'clock.
It's eleven o'clock.
It's twelve o'clock.

It's three o'clock.
It's eight o'clock.

Exercise 5 Seite 63

München
10.22 Uhr

What time is it?

It's ten o'clock.

Exercise 6 Seite 64
It's twelve o'clock.
It's three o'clock.
It's ten o'clock.

TEST

Höchstpunktzahl: **16 Punkte**

Exercise 1 Seite 65
Zähle für jedes richtig angekreuzte
Wort **1 Punkt**.
pig   sheep
dog   cat

Exercise 2 Seite 65
Zähle für jeden richtig eingesetzten
Buchstaben **1 Punkt**.
a brown horse
a red bird
a yellow chicken

Exercise 3 Seite 66
Zähle für jede richtig aufgefüllte
Lücke **1 Punkt**.
Mon → Monday
Tue → Tuesday
Wed → Wednesday
Thurs → Thursday
Fri → Friday
Sat → Saturday
Sun → Sunday

Exercise 4   Seite 66

Zähle für jede richtige Zuordnung
1 Punkt.

a) It's one o'clock.

b) It's five o'clock.

c) It's seven o'clock.

d) It's ten o'clock.

TESTAUSWERTUNG

16–13 Punkte

Gratulation! Du hast die Testaufgaben prima gelöst!

12–10 Punkte

Gut! Du hast schon ziemlich viele Punkte zusammen. Schaffst du es, noch konzentrierter zu arbeiten?

9–7 Punkte

Du hast etwa die Hälfte der Punkte erreicht. Das ist schon ganz gut. Schau dir aber nochmals an, was dir Schwierigkeiten bereitet hat, und wiederhole schwierige Aufgaben.

6–4 Punkte

Du hast schon einiges gelernt, doch mit manchen Aufgaben scheinst du noch Probleme zu haben. Sieh dir diese Übungen nochmals gut an. Vielleicht kannst du jemanden bitten, dir zu helfen?

unter 3 Punkte

Bitte deine Eltern, dir die Aufgaben nochmals zu erklären, und wiederhole regelmäßig. Du weißt ja: Übung macht den Meister!